Pebble® Plus

SEA LIFE

SEA LIONS

by **Elizabeth R. Johnson**

Raintree is an imprint of Capstone Global Library Limited, a company incorporated in England and Wales having its registered office at 264 Banbury Road, Oxford, OX2 7DY – Registered company number: 6695582

www.raintree.co.uk
myorders@raintree.co.uk

ISBN 978 1 4747 2591 0 (hardback)
20 19 18 17 16
10 9 8 7 6 5 4 3 2 1

ISBN 978 1 4747 2595 8 (paperback)
21 20 19 18 17
10 9 8 7 6 5 4 3 2 1

British Library Cataloguing in Publication Data
A full catalogue record for this book is available from the British Library.

Editorial Credits
Jaclyn Jaycox, editor; Philippa Jenkins, designer;
Svetlana Zhurkin, media researcher; Gene Bentdahl, production specialist

Photo Credits
iStockphoto: mrbfaust, cover; Minden Pictures: Michael Quinton, 17, Michio Hoshino, 7; Shutterstock: A.F.Smith, 5, Andrey Gudkov, 9, 15, Bildagentur Zoonar GmbH, 19, chbaum, 13, Christian Musat, 11, Eric Isselee, back cover, 3, 6, 24, Longjourneys, 21

Design Elements by Shutterstock

Printed and bound in China.

Contents

Life in the ocean

Look at that sea lion gliding through the waves! There are six types of sea lion. They all live along the coast of the Pacific Ocean.

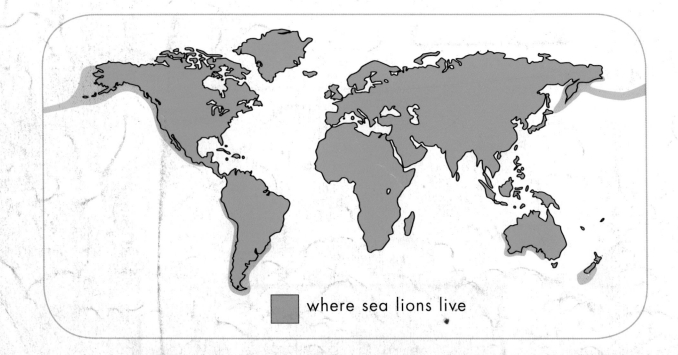

where sea lions live

Sea lions spend time in large groups. A group of sea lions in the ocean is called a raft.

Sea lions are loud!

They bark, honk and roar.

A pup knows the sound of its

mother's bark in a group.

9

Up close

Sea lions are related to seals and look like them. But they have differences too. Sea lions have ear flaps. Seals just have very small ear openings.

ear flap

Sea lions are big animals.

The largest sea lions weigh up to

1,120 kilograms (2,469 pounds)!

13

Sea lions are strong swimmers. They use flippers to swim and walk. A sea lion's coat is waterproof. Underneath the coat is a thick layer of blubber.

flippers

Finding food

Sea lions eat fish and squid.
They also like crabs and clams.
Sea lions dive deep under water
to find food. They can hold their
breath for 10 to 20 minutes!

Life cycle

Sea lions leave the ocean to mate and give birth. Newborn pups drink their mother's milk. They have a fuzzy coat of fur to keep them warm.

After a few weeks, pups learn to swim and hunt. They stay with their mother for up to one year. In the wild, sea lions live for up to 30 years.

Glossary

blubber thick layer of fat under the skin of some animals; blubber keeps animals warm

coast land next to an ocean or sea

flipper one of the broad, flat limbs of a sea lion that helps it to swim

glide move smoothly and easily

mate join with another to produce young

waterproof able to keep water out

Read more

First Encyclopedia of Seas and Oceans, Ben Denne (Usborne Publishing, 2011)

Living and Non-Living in the Ocean (Is it Living or Non-Living?), Rebecca Rissman (Raintree, 2014)

Ocean Food Chains (Food Chains and Webs), Angela Royston (Raintree, 2014)

Websites

www.bbc.co.uk/nature/life/Pinniped
Discover more about walruses, seals and sea lions.

www.dkfindout.com/uk/animals-and-nature/seals-sea-lions-and-walruses/
Learn more about sea lions and other ocean animals.

Index